Thomas Edison

by Lola M. Schaefer

Consulting Editor: Gail Saunders-Smith, Ph.D.

Consultant: Douglas Tarr, Reference Archivist,
Edison National Historic Site
West Orange, New Jersey

Pebble Books

an imprint of Capstone Press
Mankato, Minnesota

Pebble Books are published by Capstone Press
151 Good Counsel Drive, P.O. Box 669, Mankato, Minnesota 56002
http://www.capstone-press.com

1 2 3 4 5 6 07 06 05 04 03 02

Library of Congress Cataloging-in-Publication Data
Schaefer, Lola M., 1950–
    Thomas Edison / by Lola M. Schaefer.
    p. cm.—(First biographies)
    Summary: Simple text and photographs present the life of Thomas Edison, the
inventor of the phonograph, lightbulb, and movies with sound.
    Includes bibliographical references and index.
    ISBN 0-7368-1436-1 (hardcover)
    ISBN 0-7368-9414-4 (paperback)
    1. Edison, Thomas A. (Thomas Alva), 1847–1931—Juvenile literature.
2. Inventors—United States—Biography—Juvenile literature. 3. Electric engineers—
United States—Biography—Juvenile literature. [1. Edison, Thomas A. (Thomas Alva),
1847–1931. 2. Inventors.] I. Title. II. First biographies (Mankato, Minn.)
TK140.E3 S33 2003
621.3'092—dc21   2002001218

Note to Parents and Teachers

The First Biographies series supports national history standards for
units on people and culture. This book describes and illustrates the
life of Thomas Edison. The images support early readers in
understanding the text. This book also introduces early readers to
subject-specific vocabulary words, which are defined in the Words
to Know section. Early readers may need assistance to read some
words and to use the Table of Contents, Words to Know, Read
More, Internet Sites, and Index/Word List sections of the book.

Table of Contents

Time Line

1847
born

Thomas Edison was born in Ohio in 1847. Thomas was a curious child. He asked many questions.

 birthplace of Thomas in Milan, Ohio

Time Line

1847
born

Thomas tried to find
answers to his questions.
He read science books.
He did experiments.
He invented new machines.

Thomas at about age 8

Time Line

1847
born

1859
sells food
on trains

8

Thomas sold food and newspapers on a train when he was 12. He set up a small laboratory in one of the train cars. Thomas tried new experiments there.

Thomas at about age 14

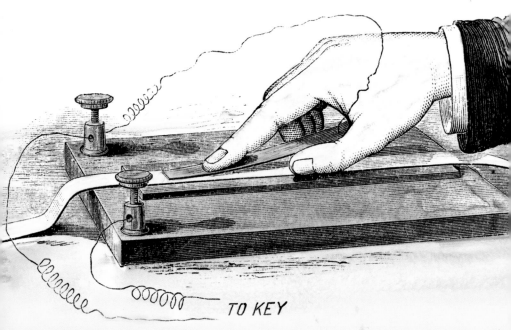

TO KEY

Time Line

1847	1859	1863
born	sells food on trains	learns to send telegraph messages

In 1863, Thomas learned how to send and receive telegraph messages. He soon invented better telegraph machines.

part of a telegraph machine

Time Line

1847 born	1859 sells food on trains	1863 learns to send telegraph messages	1876 moves to Menlo Park

In 1876, Thomas moved
to Menlo Park, New Jersey.
Thomas built a large
laboratory. He asked
other good scientists
to work with him.

◀ Thomas's laboratory in Menlo Park, New Jersey

Time Line

| 1847 born | 1859 sells food on trains | 1863 learns to send telegraph messages | 1876 moves to Menlo Park |

Thomas worked hard
in his laboratory.
In 1877, he improved
the telephone. He also
invented the phonograph.

◀ Thomas with a phonograph

1877
invents
phonograph

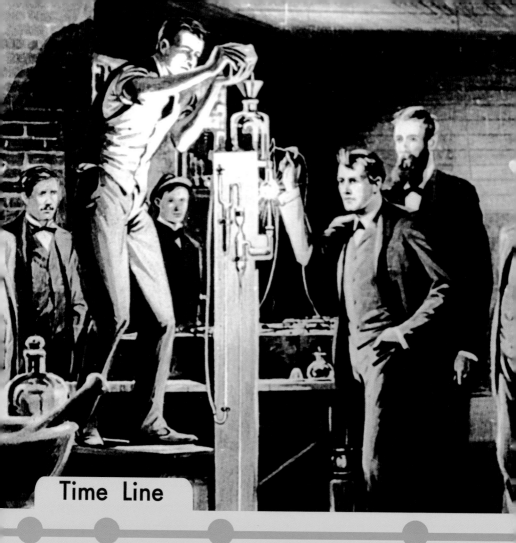

Time Line

1847
born

1859
sells food
on trains

1863
learns to send
telegraph messages

1876
moves to
Menlo Park

Thomas wanted to make a light that ran by electricity. He tried more than 1,000 lights. In 1879, he found one that worked. He invented the lightbulb.

Thomas lighting a lightbulb

1877
invents
phonograph

1879
invents electric
lightbulb

Time Line

1847
born

1859
sells food
on trains

1863
learns to send
telegraph messages

1876
moves to
Menlo Park

18

Thomas made many other inventions. He invented a movie camera. He invented a type of copy machine. People called him the "Wizard of Menlo Park."

Thomas with a movie camera

1877
invents
phonograph

1879
invents electric
lightbulb

1893
invents a
movie camera

Time Line

| 1847 born | 1859 sells food on trains | 1863 learns to send telegraph messages | 1876 moves to Menlo Park |

Thomas Edison was one of the greatest American inventors. He died in 1931. People around the world still use his inventions today.

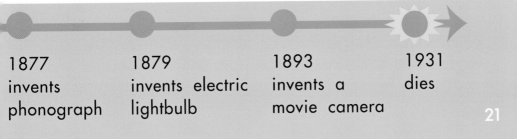

1877
invents
phonograph

1879
invents electric
lightbulb

1893
invents a
movie camera

1931
dies

Words to Know

camera—a machine for taking photographs or making movies

electricity—a form of energy

experiment—a test to learn something new

invent—to think of and create something new; Thomas Edison invented more than 1,000 items.

laboratory—a room or building with special equipment for people to use in scientific experiments

phonograph—a machine that plays sounds that have been recorded in the grooves of a record; a record has recorded sound or music.

science—the study of nature and the physical world by testing, doing experiments, and measuring

telegraph—a machine that uses electrical signals to send messages over long distances

Read More

Gaines, Ann. *Thomas Edison.* Discover the Life of an Inventor. Vero Beach, Fla.: Rourke Books, 2002.

Linder, Greg. *Thomas Edison: A Photo-Illustrated Biography.* Mankato, Minn.: Bridgestone Books, 1999.

Mason, Paul. *Thomas A. Edison.* Scientists Who Made History. Austin, Texas: Raintree Steck-Vaughn, 2002.

Shuter, Jane. *Thomas Edison.* Lives and Times. Chicago: Heinemann Library, 2000.

Internet Sites

Edison National Historic Site
http://www.nps.gov/edis

Edison's Miracle of Light
http://www.pbs.org/wgbh/amex/edison

Edison: The Wizard of Menlo Park
http://www.edisonnj.org/menlopark/taemenlo.asp

Thomas Alva Edison
http://www.americasstory.com/cgi-bin/page.cgi/aa/edison

Index/Word List

Word Count: 196
Early-Intervention Level: 20

Editorial Credits
Martha E. H. Rustad, editor; Heather Kindseth, series designer; Linda Clavel, illustrator; Patrick D. Dentinger, book designer; Wanda Winch, photo researcher; Karen Risch, product planning editor

Photo Credits
Corbis, 6
Hulton/Archive by Getty Images, cover, 14, 16
North Wind Picture Archives, 10, 18
U.S. Department of the Interior, National Park Service, Edison National Historic Site, 1, 4, 8, 12, 20